50 Perfect Cakes for Birthdays and Celebrations

By: Kelly Johnson

Table of Contents

- Classic Vanilla Birthday Cake
- Chocolate Fudge Celebration Cake
- Funfetti Cake
- Red Velvet Cake
- Lemon Raspberry Layer Cake
- Cheesecake with Fruit Topping
- Carrot Cake with Cream Cheese Frosting
- Rainbow Layer Cake
- Mocha Cake
- Almond Cake with Buttercream Frosting
- Strawberry Shortcake
- Pineapple Upside-Down Cake
- Chocolate Lava Cake
- Tiramisu Cake
- Blueberry Lemon Cake
- Vanilla Bean Cake with Buttercream
- Champagne Cake
- Coconut Cream Cake
- Apple Spice Cake
- German Chocolate Cake
- Chocolate Mousse Cake
- Cookie Monster Cake
- Cookies and Cream Cake
- Lemon Meringue Cake
- S'mores Cake
- Mango Coconut Cake
- Hazelnut Chocolate Cake
- Pina Colada Cake
- Raspberry Almond Cake
- Funfetti Cupcake Cake
- Strawberry Cheesecake Cake
- Pumpkin Spice Cake
- Mocha Espresso Cake
- Coconut Pineapple Cake
- Chocolate Mint Cake

- White Chocolate Raspberry Cake
- Black Forest Cake
- Cotton Candy Cake
- Churro Cake
- Blue Velvet Cake
- Peanut Butter Chocolate Cake
- Nutella Swirl Cake
- Chocoholic's Dream Cake
- Caramel Pecan Cake
- Matcha Green Tea Cake
- Peanut Butter Cup Cake
- Lemon Buttercream Cake
- Sweet Potato Cake
- Pistachio Rose Cake
- Marble Cake

Classic Vanilla Birthday Cake

Ingredients:

- 2 1/2 cups all-purpose flour
- 2 1/2 tsp baking powder
- 1/2 tsp salt
- 1 cup unsalted butter, softened
- 2 cups granulated sugar
- 4 large eggs
- 1 tbsp vanilla extract
- 1 cup whole milk

Instructions:

1. Preheat oven to 350°F (175°C). Grease and flour two 9-inch round cake pans.
2. In a bowl, whisk together flour, baking powder, and salt.
3. In a separate bowl, beat butter and sugar until light and fluffy. Add eggs one at a time, then stir in vanilla extract.
4. Gradually add the dry ingredients to the wet mixture, alternating with milk, and mix until smooth.
5. Divide the batter evenly between the prepared pans and bake for 30-35 minutes, until a toothpick inserted comes out clean.
6. Let the cakes cool completely before frosting with buttercream or your favorite frosting.

Chocolate Fudge Celebration Cake

Ingredients:

- 1 3/4 cups all-purpose flour
- 1 1/2 cups granulated sugar
- 3/4 cup unsweetened cocoa powder
- 1 1/2 tsp baking powder
- 1 1/2 tsp baking soda
- 1 tsp salt
- 2 large eggs
- 1 cup whole milk
- 1/2 cup vegetable oil
- 2 tsp vanilla extract
- 1 cup boiling water
- 1 cup sour cream

Instructions:

1. Preheat oven to 350°F (175°C). Grease and flour two 9-inch round cake pans.
2. In a large bowl, whisk together flour, sugar, cocoa, baking powder, baking soda, and salt.
3. Add eggs, milk, oil, and vanilla. Beat until smooth. Stir in the sour cream.
4. Gradually add the boiling water and mix until combined. The batter will be thin.
5. Pour batter into prepared pans and bake for 30-35 minutes.
6. Let cool completely before frosting with chocolate fudge frosting.

Funfetti Cake

Ingredients:

- 2 1/2 cups all-purpose flour
- 2 1/2 tsp baking powder
- 1/2 tsp salt
- 1 cup unsalted butter, softened
- 1 1/2 cups granulated sugar
- 4 large eggs
- 1 tbsp vanilla extract
- 1 cup whole milk
- 1/2 cup rainbow sprinkles

Instructions:

1. Preheat oven to 350°F (175°C). Grease and flour two 9-inch round cake pans.
2. In a bowl, whisk together flour, baking powder, and salt.
3. In a separate bowl, beat butter and sugar until light and fluffy. Add eggs one at a time, then stir in vanilla extract.
4. Gradually add the dry ingredients to the wet mixture, alternating with milk, and mix until smooth.
5. Gently fold in the sprinkles.
6. Divide the batter evenly between the pans and bake for 25-30 minutes.
7. Let cool completely before frosting with vanilla buttercream and more sprinkles.

Red Velvet Cake

Ingredients:

- 2 1/2 cups all-purpose flour
- 1 1/2 cups granulated sugar
- 1 tbsp cocoa powder
- 1 1/2 tsp baking soda
- 1 tsp salt
- 1 cup buttermilk
- 1/2 cup vegetable oil
- 2 large eggs
- 2 tbsp red food coloring
- 1 tsp vanilla extract
- 1 tsp white vinegar

Instructions:

1. Preheat oven to 350°F (175°C). Grease and flour two 9-inch round cake pans.
2. In a bowl, whisk together flour, sugar, cocoa powder, baking soda, and salt.
3. In a separate bowl, whisk together buttermilk, oil, eggs, food coloring, vanilla, and vinegar.
4. Gradually add the wet ingredients to the dry ingredients and mix until smooth.
5. Divide the batter evenly between the pans and bake for 30-35 minutes.
6. Let cool completely before frosting with cream cheese frosting.

Lemon Raspberry Layer Cake

Ingredients:

- 2 1/2 cups all-purpose flour
- 1 1/2 tsp baking powder
- 1/2 tsp baking soda
- 1/2 tsp salt
- 1/2 cup unsalted butter, softened
- 1 1/2 cups granulated sugar
- 3 large eggs
- 1/2 cup sour cream
- 1/2 cup lemon juice
- 1 tbsp lemon zest
- 1 1/2 cups fresh raspberries

Instructions:

1. Preheat oven to 350°F (175°C). Grease and flour two 9-inch round cake pans.
2. In a bowl, whisk together flour, baking powder, baking soda, and salt.
3. In a separate bowl, beat butter and sugar until light and fluffy. Add eggs one at a time.
4. Add sour cream, lemon juice, and zest, then gradually add the dry ingredients and mix until smooth.
5. Gently fold in raspberries.
6. Divide the batter between the pans and bake for 30-35 minutes.
7. Let cool before frosting with lemon cream cheese frosting.

Cheesecake with Fruit Topping

Ingredients for the crust:

- 1 1/2 cups graham cracker crumbs
- 1/4 cup granulated sugar
- 1/2 cup unsalted butter, melted

Ingredients for the filling:

- 3 (8 oz) packages cream cheese, softened
- 1 cup granulated sugar
- 3 large eggs
- 1 tsp vanilla extract
- 1 cup sour cream

Ingredients for the topping:

- 2 cups mixed fresh fruit (berries, peaches, etc.)

Instructions:

1. Preheat oven to 325°F (163°C). Grease and line a 9-inch springform pan.
2. For the crust, combine graham cracker crumbs, sugar, and melted butter. Press into the bottom of the pan.
3. For the filling, beat cream cheese and sugar until smooth. Add eggs one at a time, then stir in vanilla extract.
4. Pour filling over the crust and bake for 55-60 minutes, until the center is set.
5. Let cool, then refrigerate for at least 4 hours before adding the fresh fruit topping.

Carrot Cake with Cream Cheese Frosting

Ingredients for the cake:

- 2 1/2 cups all-purpose flour
- 1 1/2 tsp baking powder
- 1 1/2 tsp baking soda
- 1 tsp ground cinnamon
- 1/2 tsp ground nutmeg
- 1/2 tsp salt
- 4 large eggs
- 1 1/2 cups vegetable oil
- 1 1/2 cups granulated sugar
- 1/2 cup brown sugar
- 2 cups grated carrots
- 1/2 cup chopped walnuts (optional)

Ingredients for the frosting:

- 8 oz cream cheese, softened
- 1/4 cup unsalted butter, softened
- 2 cups powdered sugar
- 1 tsp vanilla extract

Instructions:

1. Preheat oven to 350°F (175°C). Grease and flour two 9-inch round cake pans.
2. In a bowl, whisk together flour, baking powder, baking soda, cinnamon, nutmeg, and salt.
3. In a separate bowl, beat eggs, oil, sugar, and brown sugar until smooth. Gradually add the dry ingredients.
4. Stir in grated carrots and walnuts (if using).
5. Divide the batter between the pans and bake for 30-35 minutes.
6. Let cool before frosting with cream cheese frosting made by beating cream cheese, butter, powdered sugar, and vanilla.

Rainbow Layer Cake

Ingredients:

- 2 1/2 cups all-purpose flour
- 1 1/2 tsp baking powder
- 1/2 tsp salt
- 1 cup unsalted butter, softened
- 2 cups granulated sugar
- 6 large eggs
- 1 tbsp vanilla extract
- 1 cup whole milk
- Food coloring (red, orange, yellow, green, blue, purple)

Instructions:

1. Preheat oven to 350°F (175°C). Grease and flour six 6-inch cake pans.
2. In a bowl, whisk together flour, baking powder, and salt.
3. In a separate bowl, beat butter and sugar until light and fluffy. Add eggs one at a time, then stir in vanilla.
4. Gradually add the dry ingredients to the wet ingredients, alternating with milk.
5. Divide the batter evenly between six bowls and tint each with a different color.
6. Pour each colored batter into a prepared cake pan and bake for 15-20 minutes, until a toothpick comes out clean.
7. Let the cakes cool before stacking and frosting with buttercream or whipped cream.

Mocha Cake

Ingredients:

- 2 cups all-purpose flour
- 1 1/2 tsp baking powder
- 1/2 tsp baking soda
- 1/4 tsp salt
- 1/2 cup unsweetened cocoa powder
- 1 cup brewed coffee (cooled)
- 1 1/2 cups granulated sugar
- 1/2 cup unsalted butter, softened
- 2 large eggs
- 1 tsp vanilla extract
- 1/2 cup sour cream

Instructions:

1. Preheat oven to 350°F (175°C). Grease and flour two 9-inch round cake pans.
2. In a bowl, whisk together flour, baking powder, baking soda, salt, and cocoa powder.
3. In a separate bowl, beat sugar and butter until light and fluffy. Add eggs one at a time, then stir in vanilla extract.
4. Gradually add the dry ingredients to the wet mixture, alternating with coffee and sour cream, and mix until smooth.
5. Divide the batter between the pans and bake for 25-30 minutes.
6. Let the cakes cool completely before frosting with coffee-flavored buttercream or chocolate ganache.

Almond Cake with Buttercream Frosting

Ingredients:

- 2 cups all-purpose flour
- 2 tsp baking powder
- 1/2 tsp salt
- 1/2 cup unsalted butter, softened
- 1 1/2 cups granulated sugar
- 4 large eggs
- 1 tsp almond extract
- 1 cup whole milk

Ingredients for Buttercream Frosting:

- 1 cup unsalted butter, softened
- 3-4 cups powdered sugar
- 2 tbsp heavy cream
- 1 tsp vanilla extract
- 1 tsp almond extract

Instructions:

1. Preheat oven to 350°F (175°C). Grease and flour two 9-inch round cake pans.
2. In a bowl, whisk together flour, baking powder, and salt.
3. In a separate bowl, beat butter and sugar until light and fluffy. Add eggs one at a time, then stir in almond extract.
4. Gradually add the dry ingredients to the wet mixture, alternating with milk, and mix until smooth.
5. Divide the batter between the pans and bake for 25-30 minutes.
6. Let the cakes cool before frosting with buttercream made by beating butter, powdered sugar, heavy cream, vanilla, and almond extract until smooth.

Strawberry Shortcake

Ingredients:

- 2 cups all-purpose flour
- 1/4 cup granulated sugar
- 1 tbsp baking powder
- 1/4 tsp salt
- 1/2 cup unsalted butter, chilled and cubed
- 2/3 cup whole milk
- 1 tsp vanilla extract
- 2 cups fresh strawberries, sliced
- 1/4 cup powdered sugar
- 1 cup heavy cream (for whipping)

Instructions:

1. Preheat oven to 400°F (200°C). Grease and flour a 9-inch round cake pan.
2. In a bowl, whisk together flour, sugar, baking powder, and salt. Add butter and cut it in until the mixture resembles coarse crumbs.
3. Stir in milk and vanilla extract, mixing until just combined. Turn the dough out onto a floured surface and knead lightly. Roll out to 1-inch thick and cut into circles.
4. Place the dough circles in the pan and bake for 15-20 minutes until golden.
5. While the cake cools, whip heavy cream with powdered sugar until stiff peaks form.
6. Slice the shortcake into halves, top with strawberries and whipped cream.

Pineapple Upside-Down Cake

Ingredients:

- 1/2 cup unsalted butter, melted
- 1 cup packed brown sugar
- 1 can (20 oz) pineapple slices, drained (reserve juice)
- Maraschino cherries (optional)
- 1 1/2 cups all-purpose flour
- 2 tsp baking powder
- 1/4 tsp salt
- 1/2 cup unsalted butter, softened
- 1 cup granulated sugar
- 2 large eggs
- 1 tsp vanilla extract
- 1/2 cup milk

Instructions:

1. Preheat oven to 350°F (175°C). Grease and line a 9-inch round cake pan.
2. Pour melted butter into the bottom of the pan, then sprinkle brown sugar evenly. Arrange pineapple slices in the pan and place cherries in the centers if using.
3. In a bowl, whisk together flour, baking powder, and salt.
4. In a separate bowl, beat butter and sugar until light and fluffy. Add eggs one at a time, then stir in vanilla extract.
5. Gradually add the dry ingredients to the wet mixture, alternating with milk, and mix until smooth.
6. Pour the batter over the pineapple slices and bake for 35-40 minutes.
7. Let the cake cool slightly, then invert onto a plate to serve.

Chocolate Lava Cake

Ingredients:

- 1/2 cup unsalted butter
- 6 oz bittersweet chocolate, chopped
- 1/4 cup granulated sugar
- 2 large eggs
- 2 large egg yolks
- 1 tsp vanilla extract
- 1/4 cup all-purpose flour
- Pinch of salt
- Powdered sugar (for dusting)

Instructions:

1. Preheat oven to 425°F (220°C). Grease and flour 4 ramekins.
2. In a bowl, melt butter and chocolate together in the microwave or on a double boiler. Stir until smooth.
3. In a separate bowl, whisk together sugar, eggs, egg yolks, and vanilla extract until light and fluffy.
4. Add the melted chocolate mixture and stir until combined. Gently fold in flour and salt.
5. Divide the batter evenly among the ramekins and bake for 12-14 minutes, until the edges are set but the center is still soft.
6. Let the cakes rest for 1-2 minutes, then invert onto plates and dust with powdered sugar.

Tiramisu Cake

Ingredients for the cake:

- 2 cups all-purpose flour
- 1 1/2 tsp baking powder
- 1/2 tsp salt
- 1 cup unsalted butter, softened
- 1 1/2 cups granulated sugar
- 3 large eggs
- 1 tsp vanilla extract
- 1/2 cup whole milk
- 1/2 cup brewed coffee, cooled

Ingredients for the filling:

- 8 oz mascarpone cheese
- 1 1/2 cups heavy cream
- 1/4 cup powdered sugar
- 2 tbsp coffee liqueur (optional)

Instructions:

1. Preheat oven to 350°F (175°C). Grease and flour two 9-inch round cake pans.
2. In a bowl, whisk together flour, baking powder, and salt.
3. In a separate bowl, beat butter and sugar until fluffy. Add eggs one at a time, then stir in vanilla extract.
4. Gradually add the dry ingredients to the wet mixture, alternating with milk and coffee, and mix until smooth.
5. Pour the batter into the pans and bake for 25-30 minutes.
6. Whip the mascarpone cheese, heavy cream, powdered sugar, and coffee liqueur (if using) until stiff peaks form.
7. Once the cakes have cooled, layer them with the mascarpone filling and refrigerate before serving.

Blueberry Lemon Cake

Ingredients:

- 2 1/2 cups all-purpose flour
- 2 tsp baking powder
- 1/2 tsp salt
- 1/2 cup unsalted butter, softened
- 1 1/2 cups granulated sugar
- 3 large eggs
- 1 tbsp lemon zest
- 1/2 cup fresh lemon juice
- 1 cup whole milk
- 1 1/2 cups fresh blueberries

Instructions:

1. Preheat oven to 350°F (175°C). Grease and flour two 9-inch round cake pans.
2. In a bowl, whisk together flour, baking powder, and salt.
3. In a separate bowl, beat butter and sugar until light and fluffy. Add eggs one at a time, then stir in lemon zest and juice.
4. Gradually add the dry ingredients to the wet mixture, alternating with milk, and mix until smooth.
5. Gently fold in blueberries.
6. Divide the batter between the pans and bake for 25-30 minutes.
7. Let the cakes cool before frosting with lemon buttercream or whipped cream.

Vanilla Bean Cake with Buttercream

Ingredients:

- 2 1/2 cups all-purpose flour
- 2 tsp baking powder
- 1/2 tsp salt
- 1 cup unsalted butter, softened
- 2 cups granulated sugar
- 4 large eggs
- 1 tbsp vanilla bean paste (or 1 vanilla bean, scraped)
- 1 cup whole milk

Instructions:

1. Preheat oven to 350°F (175°C). Grease and flour two 9-inch round cake pans.
2. In a bowl, whisk together flour, baking powder, and salt.
3. In a separate bowl, beat butter and sugar until fluffy. Add eggs one at a time, then stir in vanilla bean paste.
4. Gradually add the dry ingredients to the wet mixture, alternating with milk, and mix until smooth.
5. Divide the batter between the pans and bake for 25-30 minutes.
6. Let the cakes cool completely before frosting with vanilla buttercream.

Champagne Cake

Ingredients:

- 1 1/2 cups champagne (or sparkling wine)
- 2 cups all-purpose flour
- 1 1/2 tsp baking powder
- 1/4 tsp salt
- 1 cup unsalted butter, softened
- 2 cups granulated sugar
- 5 large eggs
- 1 tsp vanilla extract

Instructions:

1. Preheat oven to 350°F (175°C). Grease and flour two 9-inch round cake pans.
2. In a bowl, whisk together flour, baking powder, and salt.
3. In a separate bowl, beat butter and sugar until light and fluffy. Add eggs one at a time, then stir in vanilla extract.
4. Gradually add the dry ingredients to the wet mixture, alternating with champagne, and mix until smooth.
5. Pour the batter into the pans and bake for 30-35 minutes.
6. Let the cakes cool before frosting with champagne buttercream or whipped cream.

Coconut Cream Cake

Ingredients:

- 2 1/2 cups all-purpose flour
- 1 1/2 tsp baking powder
- 1/2 tsp salt
- 1 cup unsalted butter, softened
- 1 1/2 cups granulated sugar
- 4 large eggs
- 1 cup coconut milk
- 1 tsp vanilla extract
- 1 cup shredded coconut (sweetened or unsweetened)

Ingredients for the Frosting:

- 1 1/2 cups heavy cream
- 1/4 cup powdered sugar
- 1 tsp vanilla extract
- 1 cup shredded coconut

Instructions:

1. Preheat oven to 350°F (175°C). Grease and flour two 9-inch round cake pans.
2. In a bowl, whisk together flour, baking powder, and salt.
3. In a separate bowl, beat butter and sugar until light and fluffy. Add eggs one at a time, then stir in coconut milk and vanilla extract.
4. Gradually add the dry ingredients to the wet mixture and mix until smooth.
5. Fold in the shredded coconut, then divide the batter between the pans and bake for 25-30 minutes.
6. Let the cakes cool before frosting with whipped cream made by beating heavy cream, powdered sugar, and vanilla extract until stiff peaks form. Garnish with extra shredded coconut.

Apple Spice Cake

Ingredients:

- 2 1/2 cups all-purpose flour
- 1 tsp cinnamon
- 1/2 tsp nutmeg
- 1 tsp baking soda
- 1/2 tsp salt
- 1/2 cup unsalted butter, softened
- 1 1/2 cups granulated sugar
- 2 large eggs
- 1 tsp vanilla extract
- 1 cup unsweetened applesauce
- 1 1/2 cups peeled and chopped apples (Granny Smith or Honeycrisp)

Instructions:

1. Preheat oven to 350°F (175°C). Grease and flour two 9-inch round cake pans.
2. In a bowl, whisk together flour, cinnamon, nutmeg, baking soda, and salt.
3. In a separate bowl, beat butter and sugar until light and fluffy. Add eggs one at a time, then stir in vanilla extract and applesauce.
4. Gradually add the dry ingredients to the wet mixture and mix until smooth.
5. Fold in the chopped apples and divide the batter between the pans. Bake for 30-35 minutes.
6. Let the cakes cool before frosting with cream cheese frosting or a dusting of powdered sugar.

German Chocolate Cake

Ingredients:

- 2 cups all-purpose flour
- 1 1/2 tsp baking powder
- 1/2 tsp baking soda
- 1/2 tsp salt
- 1 cup unsweetened cocoa powder
- 1 cup unsalted butter, softened
- 1 1/2 cups granulated sugar
- 4 large eggs
- 1 tsp vanilla extract
- 1 cup buttermilk
- 1 cup boiling water

Ingredients for the Frosting:

- 1 cup heavy cream
- 1 cup brown sugar, packed
- 1/2 cup unsalted butter
- 1 cup sweetened shredded coconut
- 1 cup chopped pecans

Instructions:

1. Preheat oven to 350°F (175°C). Grease and flour two 9-inch round cake pans.
2. In a bowl, whisk together flour, baking powder, baking soda, salt, and cocoa powder.
3. In a separate bowl, beat butter and sugar until light and fluffy. Add eggs one at a time, then stir in vanilla extract.
4. Gradually add the dry ingredients to the wet mixture, alternating with buttermilk, and mix until smooth.
5. Stir in the boiling water to thin the batter, then pour into the prepared pans. Bake for 30-35 minutes.
6. For the frosting, combine heavy cream, brown sugar, and butter in a saucepan over medium heat. Bring to a simmer and cook for 5 minutes. Remove from heat, then stir in coconut and pecans.
7. Let the cakes cool completely before frosting.

Chocolate Mousse Cake

Ingredients for the cake:

- 1 1/2 cups all-purpose flour
- 1 1/2 tsp baking powder
- 1/2 cup unsweetened cocoa powder
- 1/4 tsp salt
- 1 cup unsalted butter, softened
- 1 1/2 cups granulated sugar
- 3 large eggs
- 1 tsp vanilla extract
- 1 cup milk

Ingredients for the mousse filling:

- 1 1/2 cups heavy cream
- 8 oz semi-sweet chocolate, chopped
- 1 tsp vanilla extract

Instructions:

1. Preheat oven to 350°F (175°C). Grease and flour two 9-inch round cake pans.
2. In a bowl, whisk together flour, baking powder, cocoa powder, and salt.
3. In a separate bowl, beat butter and sugar until light and fluffy. Add eggs one at a time, then stir in vanilla extract.
4. Gradually add the dry ingredients to the wet mixture, alternating with milk, and mix until smooth.
5. Divide the batter between the pans and bake for 25-30 minutes.
6. For the mousse, heat the cream in a saucepan until simmering, then pour over the chopped chocolate. Let it sit for 5 minutes, then stir until smooth. Stir in vanilla extract.
7. Let the mousse cool, then spread it between the cooled cake layers.

Cookie Monster Cake

Ingredients:

- 2 1/2 cups all-purpose flour
- 1 1/2 tsp baking powder
- 1/2 tsp baking soda
- 1/4 tsp salt
- 1 cup unsalted butter, softened
- 1 1/2 cups granulated sugar
- 2 large eggs
- 1 tsp vanilla extract
- 1 cup sour cream

Ingredients for the frosting:

- 1 cup unsalted butter, softened
- 4 cups powdered sugar
- 2-3 tbsp heavy cream
- Blue food coloring
- Mini chocolate chip cookies (for decoration)

Instructions:

1. Preheat oven to 350°F (175°C). Grease and flour two 9-inch round cake pans.
2. In a bowl, whisk together flour, baking powder, baking soda, and salt.
3. In a separate bowl, beat butter and sugar until light and fluffy. Add eggs one at a time, then stir in vanilla extract.
4. Gradually add the dry ingredients to the wet mixture, alternating with sour cream, and mix until smooth.
5. Divide the batter between the pans and bake for 25-30 minutes.
6. For the frosting, beat butter and powdered sugar until fluffy, then add heavy cream and blue food coloring until the desired shade is reached.
7. Frost the cakes and decorate with mini chocolate chip cookies for a "cookie monster" effect.

Cookies and Cream Cake

Ingredients for the cake:

- 2 cups all-purpose flour
- 1 1/2 tsp baking powder
- 1/2 tsp baking soda
- 1/2 tsp salt
- 1/2 cup unsweetened cocoa powder
- 1 cup unsalted butter, softened
- 1 1/2 cups granulated sugar
- 2 large eggs
- 1 tsp vanilla extract
- 1 cup milk
- 1 cup crushed Oreos (or similar sandwich cookies)

Ingredients for the frosting:

- 1 cup unsalted butter, softened
- 4 cups powdered sugar
- 2-3 tbsp heavy cream
- 1 tsp vanilla extract
- 1 cup crushed Oreos

Instructions:

1. Preheat oven to 350°F (175°C). Grease and flour two 9-inch round cake pans.
2. In a bowl, whisk together flour, baking powder, baking soda, salt, and cocoa powder.
3. In a separate bowl, beat butter and sugar until light and fluffy. Add eggs one at a time, then stir in vanilla extract.
4. Gradually add the dry ingredients to the wet mixture, alternating with milk, and mix until smooth.
5. Fold in crushed Oreos, then divide the batter between the pans and bake for 25-30 minutes.
6. For the frosting, beat butter and powdered sugar until fluffy, then add heavy cream and vanilla extract. Stir in crushed Oreos.
7. Frost the cakes and garnish with extra crushed Oreos.

Lemon Meringue Cake

Ingredients for the cake:

- 2 1/2 cups all-purpose flour
- 2 tsp baking powder
- 1/4 tsp salt
- 1 cup unsalted butter, softened
- 1 1/2 cups granulated sugar
- 4 large eggs
- 1 tbsp lemon zest
- 1/2 cup lemon juice
- 1 cup buttermilk

Ingredients for the meringue:

- 4 large egg whites
- 1/4 tsp cream of tartar
- 1/2 cup granulated sugar

Instructions:

1. Preheat oven to 350°F (175°C). Grease and flour two 9-inch round cake pans.
2. In a bowl, whisk together flour, baking powder, and salt.
3. In a separate bowl, beat butter and sugar until light and fluffy. Add eggs one at a time, then stir in lemon zest and lemon juice.
4. Gradually add the dry ingredients to the wet mixture, alternating with buttermilk, and mix until smooth.
5. Divide the batter between the pans and bake for 25-30 minutes.
6. For the meringue, beat egg whites and cream of tartar until soft peaks form. Gradually add sugar and beat until stiff peaks form.
7. Frost the cooled cakes with meringue and bake in the oven at 350°F (175°C) for 5-7 minutes or until golden brown.

S'mores Cake

Ingredients for the cake:

- 2 cups all-purpose flour
- 1 1/2 tsp baking powder
- 1/2 tsp salt
- 1/2 cup unsweetened cocoa powder
- 1 cup unsalted butter, softened
- 1 1/2 cups granulated sugar
- 2 large eggs
- 1 tsp vanilla extract
- 1 cup milk
- 1/2 cup crushed graham crackers

Ingredients for the frosting:

- 1 cup unsalted butter, softened
- 4 cups powdered sugar
- 1/4 cup cocoa powder
- 1/4 cup milk
- 1 cup mini marshmallows

Instructions:

1. Preheat oven to 350°F (175°C). Grease and flour two 9-inch round cake pans.
2. In a bowl, whisk together flour, baking powder, salt, and cocoa powder.
3. In a separate bowl, beat butter and sugar until light and fluffy. Add eggs one at a time, then stir in vanilla extract.
4. Gradually add the dry ingredients to the wet mixture, alternating with milk, and mix until smooth.
5. Fold in crushed graham crackers, then divide the batter between the pans and bake for 25-30 minutes.
6. For the frosting, beat butter and powdered sugar until fluffy, then add cocoa powder and milk. Frost the cooled cakes and top with mini marshmallows.

Mango Coconut Cake

Ingredients for the cake:

- 2 1/2 cups all-purpose flour
- 1 1/2 tsp baking powder
- 1/2 tsp salt
- 1 cup unsalted butter, softened
- 1 1/2 cups granulated sugar
- 3 large eggs
- 1 cup mango puree
- 1 cup unsweetened coconut milk
- 1 tsp vanilla extract
- 1 cup shredded coconut

Ingredients for the frosting:

- 1 cup unsalted butter, softened
- 4 cups powdered sugar
- 1/4 cup coconut milk
- 1/2 cup shredded coconut

Instructions:

1. Preheat oven to 350°F (175°C). Grease and flour two 9-inch round cake pans.
2. In a bowl, whisk together flour, baking powder, and salt.
3. In a separate bowl, beat butter and sugar until light and fluffy. Add eggs one at a time, then stir in mango puree, coconut milk, and vanilla extract.
4. Gradually add the dry ingredients to the wet mixture and mix until smooth.
5. Fold in shredded coconut, then divide the batter between the pans and bake for 25-30 minutes.
6. For the frosting, beat butter and powdered sugar until smooth, then add coconut milk and mix until fluffy.
7. Frost the cooled cakes and garnish with shredded coconut.

Hazelnut Chocolate Cake

Ingredients for the cake:

- 1 1/2 cups all-purpose flour
- 1 cup unsweetened cocoa powder
- 1 1/2 tsp baking powder
- 1/2 tsp salt
- 1 cup unsalted butter, softened
- 1 1/2 cups granulated sugar
- 3 large eggs
- 1 tsp vanilla extract
- 1 cup milk
- 1 cup ground hazelnuts

Ingredients for the frosting:

- 1 cup unsalted butter, softened
- 2 cups powdered sugar
- 1/2 cup cocoa powder
- 1 tsp vanilla extract
- 1/4 cup heavy cream
- 1/2 cup chopped toasted hazelnuts

Instructions:

1. Preheat oven to 350°F (175°C). Grease and flour two 9-inch round cake pans.
2. In a bowl, whisk together flour, cocoa powder, baking powder, and salt.
3. In a separate bowl, beat butter and sugar until light and fluffy. Add eggs one at a time, then stir in vanilla extract.
4. Gradually add the dry ingredients to the wet mixture, alternating with milk, and mix until smooth.
5. Fold in ground hazelnuts, then divide the batter between the pans and bake for 25-30 minutes.
6. For the frosting, beat butter, powdered sugar, cocoa powder, and vanilla extract until smooth. Add heavy cream to reach the desired consistency.
7. Frost the cooled cakes and garnish with chopped hazelnuts.

Pina Colada Cake

Ingredients for the cake:

- 2 cups all-purpose flour
- 1 1/2 tsp baking powder
- 1/2 tsp salt
- 1 cup unsalted butter, softened
- 1 1/2 cups granulated sugar
- 4 large eggs
- 1/2 cup coconut milk
- 1/2 cup pineapple juice
- 1 tsp vanilla extract
- 1 cup shredded coconut

Ingredients for the frosting:

- 1 cup unsalted butter, softened
- 4 cups powdered sugar
- 1/4 cup pineapple juice
- 1/4 cup coconut milk
- 1/2 cup shredded coconut

Instructions:

1. Preheat oven to 350°F (175°C). Grease and flour two 9-inch round cake pans.
2. In a bowl, whisk together flour, baking powder, and salt.
3. In a separate bowl, beat butter and sugar until light and fluffy. Add eggs one at a time, then stir in coconut milk, pineapple juice, and vanilla extract.
4. Gradually add the dry ingredients to the wet mixture and mix until smooth.
5. Fold in shredded coconut, then divide the batter between the pans and bake for 25-30 minutes.
6. For the frosting, beat butter and powdered sugar until smooth. Add pineapple juice and coconut milk to achieve a creamy consistency.
7. Frost the cooled cakes and garnish with shredded coconut.

Raspberry Almond Cake

Ingredients for the cake:

- 2 1/2 cups all-purpose flour
- 1 1/2 tsp baking powder
- 1/2 tsp salt
- 1/2 cup unsalted butter, softened
- 1 1/2 cups granulated sugar
- 3 large eggs
- 1 tsp almond extract
- 1/2 cup milk
- 1 cup fresh raspberries

Ingredients for the frosting:

- 1 cup unsalted butter, softened
- 4 cups powdered sugar
- 1 tsp almond extract
- 1/4 cup milk
- 1/2 cup raspberry puree

Instructions:

1. Preheat oven to 350°F (175°C). Grease and flour two 9-inch round cake pans.
2. In a bowl, whisk together flour, baking powder, and salt.
3. In a separate bowl, beat butter and sugar until light and fluffy. Add eggs one at a time, then stir in almond extract.
4. Gradually add the dry ingredients to the wet mixture, alternating with milk, and mix until smooth.
5. Gently fold in fresh raspberries, then divide the batter between the pans and bake for 25-30 minutes.
6. For the frosting, beat butter and powdered sugar until fluffy, then add almond extract, milk, and raspberry puree.
7. Frost the cooled cakes with the raspberry almond frosting.

Funfetti Cupcake Cake

Ingredients for the cake:

- 2 1/2 cups all-purpose flour
- 1 1/2 tsp baking powder
- 1/2 tsp salt
- 1 cup unsalted butter, softened
- 1 1/2 cups granulated sugar
- 3 large eggs
- 1 tsp vanilla extract
- 1 cup milk
- 1/2 cup rainbow sprinkles

Ingredients for the frosting:

- 1 cup unsalted butter, softened
- 4 cups powdered sugar
- 2-3 tbsp heavy cream
- 1 tsp vanilla extract
- Additional rainbow sprinkles for decorating

Instructions:

1. Preheat oven to 350°F (175°C). Grease and flour a 9-inch round cake pan.
2. In a bowl, whisk together flour, baking powder, and salt.
3. In a separate bowl, beat butter and sugar until light and fluffy. Add eggs one at a time, then stir in vanilla extract.
4. Gradually add the dry ingredients to the wet mixture, alternating with milk, and mix until smooth.
5. Fold in rainbow sprinkles, then divide the batter into cupcake-sized portions or the pan, and bake for 20-25 minutes.
6. For the frosting, beat butter and powdered sugar until smooth. Add heavy cream and vanilla extract to achieve a creamy consistency.
7. Frost the cooled cake with the frosting and top with extra rainbow sprinkles.

Strawberry Cheesecake Cake

Ingredients for the cake:

- 2 1/2 cups all-purpose flour
- 1 1/2 tsp baking powder
- 1/2 tsp salt
- 1 cup unsalted butter, softened
- 1 1/2 cups granulated sugar
- 3 large eggs
- 1 cup sour cream
- 1 tsp vanilla extract

Ingredients for the cheesecake filling:

- 1 1/2 cups cream cheese, softened
- 1 cup powdered sugar
- 1 tsp vanilla extract
- 1/2 cup fresh strawberries, pureed

Ingredients for the frosting:

- 1 cup unsalted butter, softened
- 4 cups powdered sugar
- 2 tbsp milk
- 1 tsp vanilla extract
- Fresh strawberries for garnish

Instructions:

1. Preheat oven to 350°F (175°C). Grease and flour two 9-inch round cake pans.
2. In a bowl, whisk together flour, baking powder, and salt.
3. In a separate bowl, beat butter and sugar until light and fluffy. Add eggs one at a time, then stir in sour cream and vanilla extract.
4. Gradually add the dry ingredients to the wet mixture and mix until smooth.
5. For the cheesecake filling, beat cream cheese, powdered sugar, and vanilla extract until smooth. Gently fold in pureed strawberries.
6. Divide the cake batter between the pans, then spoon the cheesecake filling into the center, spreading it out. Bake for 25-30 minutes.
7. For the frosting, beat butter and powdered sugar until smooth. Add milk and vanilla extract to achieve a creamy consistency.

8. Frost the cooled cakes and garnish with fresh strawberries.

Pumpkin Spice Cake

Ingredients for the cake:

- 2 1/2 cups all-purpose flour
- 1 1/2 tsp baking powder
- 1 tsp baking soda
- 1/2 tsp salt
- 1 tsp cinnamon
- 1/2 tsp nutmeg
- 1 cup unsalted butter, softened
- 1 1/2 cups granulated sugar
- 4 large eggs
- 1 cup pumpkin puree
- 1 tsp vanilla extract

Ingredients for the frosting:

- 1 cup unsalted butter, softened
- 4 cups powdered sugar
- 2 tsp cinnamon
- 1 tsp vanilla extract
- 2 tbsp heavy cream

Instructions:

1. Preheat oven to 350°F (175°C). Grease and flour two 9-inch round cake pans.
2. In a bowl, whisk together flour, baking powder, baking soda, salt, cinnamon, and nutmeg.
3. In a separate bowl, beat butter and sugar until light and fluffy. Add eggs one at a time, then stir in pumpkin puree and vanilla extract.
4. Gradually add the dry ingredients to the wet mixture and mix until smooth.
5. Divide the batter between the pans and bake for 25-30 minutes.
6. For the frosting, beat butter and powdered sugar until smooth. Add cinnamon, vanilla extract, and heavy cream.
7. Frost the cooled cakes and serve.

Mocha Espresso Cake

Ingredients for the cake:

- 2 cups all-purpose flour
- 1 1/2 tsp baking powder
- 1/2 tsp salt
- 1/2 cup unsweetened cocoa powder
- 1 cup unsalted butter, softened
- 1 1/2 cups granulated sugar
- 3 large eggs
- 1 tsp vanilla extract
- 1/2 cup brewed espresso
- 1/2 cup milk

Ingredients for the frosting:

- 1 cup unsalted butter, softened
- 4 cups powdered sugar
- 2 tbsp brewed espresso
- 1/4 cup cocoa powder

Instructions:

1. Preheat oven to 350°F (175°C). Grease and flour two 9-inch round cake pans.
2. In a bowl, whisk together flour, baking powder, salt, and cocoa powder.
3. In a separate bowl, beat butter and sugar until light and fluffy. Add eggs one at a time, then stir in vanilla extract, brewed espresso, and milk.
4. Gradually add the dry ingredients to the wet mixture and mix until smooth.
5. Divide the batter between the pans and bake for 25-30 minutes.
6. For the frosting, beat butter and powdered sugar until smooth. Add brewed espresso and cocoa powder to achieve a creamy consistency.
7. Frost the cooled cakes and enjoy.

Coconut Pineapple Cake

Ingredients for the cake:

- 2 1/2 cups all-purpose flour
- 1 1/2 tsp baking powder
- 1/2 tsp baking soda
- 1/2 tsp salt
- 1 cup unsalted butter, softened
- 1 1/2 cups granulated sugar
- 4 large eggs
- 1 cup coconut milk
- 1/2 cup pineapple juice
- 1 cup crushed pineapple (drained)
- 1 cup shredded coconut

Ingredients for the frosting:

- 1 cup unsalted butter, softened
- 4 cups powdered sugar
- 1/4 cup coconut milk
- 1 tsp vanilla extract
- 1/2 cup shredded coconut for garnish
- Pineapple chunks for garnish

Instructions:

1. Preheat oven to 350°F (175°C). Grease and flour two 9-inch round cake pans.
2. In a bowl, whisk together flour, baking powder, baking soda, and salt.
3. In a separate bowl, beat butter and sugar until light and fluffy. Add eggs one at a time, then stir in coconut milk and pineapple juice.
4. Gradually add the dry ingredients and mix until smooth. Fold in crushed pineapple and shredded coconut.
5. Divide the batter between the pans and bake for 25-30 minutes.
6. For the frosting, beat butter and powdered sugar until smooth. Add coconut milk and vanilla extract.
7. Frost the cooled cakes and garnish with shredded coconut and pineapple chunks.

Chocolate Mint Cake

Ingredients for the cake:

- 2 cups all-purpose flour
- 1 1/2 cups unsweetened cocoa powder
- 1 1/2 tsp baking powder
- 1/2 tsp baking soda
- 1/2 tsp salt
- 1 cup unsalted butter, softened
- 1 1/2 cups granulated sugar
- 3 large eggs
- 1 tsp peppermint extract
- 1 cup buttermilk

Ingredients for the frosting:

- 1 cup unsalted butter, softened
- 4 cups powdered sugar
- 1/4 cup heavy cream
- 1 tsp peppermint extract
- Green food coloring (optional)

Instructions:

1. Preheat oven to 350°F (175°C). Grease and flour two 9-inch round cake pans.
2. In a bowl, whisk together flour, cocoa powder, baking powder, baking soda, and salt.
3. In a separate bowl, beat butter and sugar until light and fluffy. Add eggs one at a time, then stir in peppermint extract.
4. Gradually add the dry ingredients, alternating with buttermilk, and mix until smooth.
5. Divide the batter between the pans and bake for 25-30 minutes.
6. For the frosting, beat butter and powdered sugar until smooth. Add heavy cream and peppermint extract, then mix until fluffy. Add green food coloring if desired.
7. Frost the cooled cakes with the mint frosting.

White Chocolate Raspberry Cake

Ingredients for the cake:

- 2 1/2 cups all-purpose flour
- 1 1/2 tsp baking powder
- 1/2 tsp salt
- 1 cup unsalted butter, softened
- 1 1/2 cups granulated sugar
- 4 large eggs
- 1 cup buttermilk
- 1 tsp vanilla extract
- 6 oz white chocolate, melted
- 1 cup fresh raspberries

Ingredients for the frosting:

- 1 cup unsalted butter, softened
- 4 cups powdered sugar
- 4 oz white chocolate, melted
- 1/4 cup raspberry puree
- Fresh raspberries for garnish

Instructions:

1. Preheat oven to 350°F (175°C). Grease and flour two 9-inch round cake pans.
2. In a bowl, whisk together flour, baking powder, and salt.
3. In a separate bowl, beat butter and sugar until light and fluffy. Add eggs one at a time, then stir in vanilla extract and melted white chocolate.
4. Gradually add the dry ingredients, alternating with buttermilk, and mix until smooth.
5. Gently fold in fresh raspberries, then divide the batter between the pans and bake for 25-30 minutes.
6. For the frosting, beat butter and powdered sugar until smooth. Add melted white chocolate and raspberry puree.
7. Frost the cooled cakes and garnish with fresh raspberries.

Black Forest Cake

Ingredients for the cake:

- 2 cups all-purpose flour
- 1 1/2 cups unsweetened cocoa powder
- 1 1/2 tsp baking powder
- 1/2 tsp baking soda
- 1/2 tsp salt
- 1 cup unsalted butter, softened
- 1 1/2 cups granulated sugar
- 3 large eggs
- 1 tsp vanilla extract
- 1 cup buttermilk
- 1 jar (24 oz) cherry pie filling
- 1/2 cup maraschino cherries, drained and halved

Ingredients for the frosting:

- 2 cups heavy whipping cream
- 3 tbsp powdered sugar
- 1 tsp vanilla extract
- Dark chocolate shavings for garnish

Instructions:

1. Preheat oven to 350°F (175°C). Grease and flour two 9-inch round cake pans.
2. In a bowl, whisk together flour, cocoa powder, baking powder, baking soda, and salt.
3. In a separate bowl, beat butter and sugar until light and fluffy. Add eggs one at a time, then stir in vanilla extract.
4. Gradually add the dry ingredients, alternating with buttermilk, and mix until smooth.
5. Divide the batter between the pans and bake for 25-30 minutes.
6. For the frosting, beat heavy cream, powdered sugar, and vanilla extract until stiff peaks form.
7. Once the cakes have cooled, layer the cakes with whipped cream, cherry pie filling, and maraschino cherries. Garnish with dark chocolate shavings.

Cotton Candy Cake

Ingredients for the cake:

- 2 1/2 cups all-purpose flour
- 1 1/2 tsp baking powder
- 1/2 tsp salt
- 1 cup unsalted butter, softened
- 1 1/2 cups granulated sugar
- 3 large eggs
- 1 tsp vanilla extract
- 1/2 tsp cotton candy flavoring (available in candy shops)
- 1 cup milk
- Pink food coloring

Ingredients for the frosting:

- 1 cup unsalted butter, softened
- 4 cups powdered sugar
- 2 tbsp milk
- 1 tsp cotton candy flavoring
- Pink food coloring

Instructions:

1. Preheat oven to 350°F (175°C). Grease and flour two 9-inch round cake pans.
2. In a bowl, whisk together flour, baking powder, and salt.
3. In a separate bowl, beat butter and sugar until light and fluffy. Add eggs one at a time, then stir in vanilla extract and cotton candy flavoring.
4. Gradually add the dry ingredients, alternating with milk, and mix until smooth.
5. Add pink food coloring until desired color is achieved, then divide the batter between the pans and bake for 25-30 minutes.
6. For the frosting, beat butter and powdered sugar until smooth. Add milk, cotton candy flavoring, and pink food coloring.
7. Frost the cooled cakes with the cotton candy frosting.

Churro Cake

Ingredients for the cake:

- 2 cups all-purpose flour
- 1 1/2 tsp baking powder
- 1/2 tsp salt
- 1/2 tsp cinnamon
- 1 cup unsalted butter, softened
- 1 1/2 cups granulated sugar
- 3 large eggs
- 1 tsp vanilla extract
- 1 cup milk

Ingredients for the frosting:

- 1 cup unsalted butter, softened
- 4 cups powdered sugar
- 1 tsp cinnamon
- 2 tbsp heavy cream
- 1/2 tsp vanilla extract

Ingredients for garnish:

- 1/4 cup cinnamon sugar

Instructions:

1. Preheat oven to 350°F (175°C). Grease and flour two 9-inch round cake pans.
2. In a bowl, whisk together flour, baking powder, salt, and cinnamon.
3. In a separate bowl, beat butter and sugar until light and fluffy. Add eggs one at a time, then stir in vanilla extract.
4. Gradually add the dry ingredients, alternating with milk, and mix until smooth.
5. Divide the batter between the pans and bake for 25-30 minutes.
6. For the frosting, beat butter and powdered sugar until smooth. Add cinnamon, heavy cream, and vanilla extract.
7. Frost the cooled cakes, then sprinkle with cinnamon sugar for garnish.

Blue Velvet Cake

Ingredients for the cake:

- 2 1/2 cups all-purpose flour
- 1 1/2 tsp baking powder
- 1/2 tsp salt
- 1 cup unsalted butter, softened
- 1 1/2 cups granulated sugar
- 2 large eggs
- 1 tsp vanilla extract
- 1 tbsp blue food coloring
- 1 cup buttermilk

Ingredients for the frosting:

- 1 cup unsalted butter, softened
- 4 cups powdered sugar
- 2 tbsp milk
- 1 tsp vanilla extract

Instructions:

1. Preheat oven to 350°F (175°C). Grease and flour two 9-inch round cake pans.
2. In a bowl, whisk together flour, baking powder, and salt.
3. In a separate bowl, beat butter and sugar until light and fluffy. Add eggs one at a time, then stir in vanilla extract and blue food coloring.
4. Gradually add the dry ingredients, alternating with buttermilk, and mix until smooth.
5. Divide the batter between the pans and bake for 25-30 minutes.
6. For the frosting, beat butter and powdered sugar until smooth. Add milk and vanilla extract.
7. Frost the cooled cakes with the blue velvet frosting.

Peanut Butter Chocolate Cake

Ingredients for the cake:

- 2 cups all-purpose flour
- 1 1/2 tsp baking powder
- 1/2 tsp baking soda
- 1/2 tsp salt
- 1 cup unsalted butter, softened
- 1 1/2 cups granulated sugar
- 2 large eggs
- 1 cup milk
- 1/2 cup creamy peanut butter
- 1/2 cup cocoa powder

Ingredients for the frosting:

- 1 cup unsalted butter, softened
- 2 cups creamy peanut butter
- 4 cups powdered sugar
- 1/4 cup cocoa powder
- 2 tbsp milk

Instructions:

1. Preheat oven to 350°F (175°C). Grease and flour two 9-inch round cake pans.
2. In a bowl, whisk together flour, baking powder, baking soda, salt, and cocoa powder.
3. In a separate bowl, beat butter, sugar, and peanut butter until light and fluffy. Add eggs one at a time, then stir in milk.
4. Gradually add the dry ingredients and mix until smooth.
5. Divide the batter between the pans and bake for 25-30 minutes.
6. For the frosting, beat peanut butter and butter until smooth. Add powdered sugar, cocoa powder, and milk, and mix until creamy.
7. Frost the cooled cakes with the peanut butter frosting.

Nutella Swirl Cake

Ingredients for the cake:

- 2 1/2 cups all-purpose flour
- 1 1/2 tsp baking powder
- 1/2 tsp salt
- 1 cup unsalted butter, softened
- 1 1/2 cups granulated sugar
- 3 large eggs
- 1 tsp vanilla extract
- 1/2 cup milk
- 1/2 cup Nutella

Ingredients for the frosting:

- 1 cup unsalted butter, softened
- 4 cups powdered sugar
- 2 tbsp milk
- 1/4 cup Nutella

Instructions:

1. Preheat oven to 350°F (175°C). Grease and flour two 9-inch round cake pans.
2. In a bowl, whisk together flour, baking powder, and salt.
3. In a separate bowl, beat butter and sugar until light and fluffy. Add eggs one at a time, then stir in vanilla extract.
4. Gradually add the dry ingredients, alternating with milk, and mix until smooth.
5. Swirl in Nutella and bake for 25-30 minutes.
6. For the frosting, beat butter and powdered sugar until smooth. Add milk and Nutella.
7. Frost the cooled cakes with the Nutella frosting.

Chocoholic's Dream Cake

Ingredients for the cake:

- 2 cups all-purpose flour
- 1 1/2 cups granulated sugar
- 3/4 cup unsweetened cocoa powder
- 1 1/2 tsp baking powder
- 1 1/2 tsp baking soda
- 1 tsp salt
- 2 large eggs
- 1 cup buttermilk
- 1/2 cup vegetable oil
- 1 tsp vanilla extract
- 1 cup boiling water
- 1 cup chocolate chips (optional)

Ingredients for the frosting:

- 1 cup unsalted butter, softened
- 1/2 cup unsweetened cocoa powder
- 3 cups powdered sugar
- 1/2 cup milk
- 1 tsp vanilla extract
- 1/2 cup chocolate chips (for garnish)

Instructions:

1. Preheat oven to 350°F (175°C). Grease and flour two 9-inch round cake pans.
2. In a large bowl, whisk together flour, sugar, cocoa powder, baking powder, baking soda, and salt.
3. Add eggs, buttermilk, oil, and vanilla extract. Mix until smooth.
4. Gradually add boiling water, stirring until combined (batter will be thin). Optionally, fold in chocolate chips.
5. Pour batter evenly into prepared pans and bake for 30-35 minutes.
6. For the frosting, beat butter and cocoa powder until smooth. Gradually add powdered sugar, milk, and vanilla extract until desired consistency.
7. Frost the cooled cakes, topping with extra chocolate chips for garnish.

Caramel Pecan Cake

Ingredients for the cake:

- 2 cups all-purpose flour
- 1 1/2 cups granulated sugar
- 1 1/2 tsp baking powder
- 1/2 tsp baking soda
- 1/4 tsp salt
- 1 cup unsalted butter, softened
- 3 large eggs
- 1 tsp vanilla extract
- 1 cup buttermilk
- 1/2 cup chopped pecans

Ingredients for the frosting:

- 1/2 cup unsalted butter
- 1 cup brown sugar
- 1/4 cup heavy cream
- 2 cups powdered sugar
- 1/2 cup chopped pecans for garnish

Instructions:

1. Preheat oven to 350°F (175°C). Grease and flour two 9-inch round cake pans.
2. In a bowl, mix flour, sugar, baking powder, baking soda, and salt.
3. In a separate bowl, beat butter until fluffy, then add eggs one at a time. Stir in vanilla extract.
4. Gradually add the dry ingredients, alternating with buttermilk. Fold in chopped pecans.
5. Divide batter between pans and bake for 25-30 minutes.
6. For the frosting, melt butter and brown sugar in a saucepan. Stir in heavy cream and bring to a boil. Cook for 2-3 minutes, then remove from heat. Gradually add powdered sugar.
7. Frost the cooled cakes with caramel frosting, topping with extra pecans.

Matcha Green Tea Cake

Ingredients for the cake:

- 2 cups all-purpose flour
- 1 1/2 tsp baking powder
- 1/2 tsp salt
- 1 tbsp matcha powder
- 1 cup unsalted butter, softened
- 1 1/2 cups granulated sugar
- 3 large eggs
- 1 tsp vanilla extract
- 1 cup buttermilk

Ingredients for the frosting:

- 1 cup unsalted butter, softened
- 4 cups powdered sugar
- 2 tbsp matcha powder
- 2 tbsp milk

Instructions:

1. Preheat oven to 350°F (175°C). Grease and flour two 9-inch round cake pans.
2. In a bowl, whisk together flour, baking powder, salt, and matcha powder.
3. In a separate bowl, beat butter and sugar until fluffy. Add eggs one at a time, then stir in vanilla extract.
4. Gradually add dry ingredients, alternating with buttermilk, until smooth.
5. Divide batter between pans and bake for 25-30 minutes.
6. For the frosting, beat butter, powdered sugar, matcha powder, and milk until smooth.
7. Frost the cooled cakes with matcha frosting.

Peanut Butter Cup Cake

Ingredients for the cake:

- 2 cups all-purpose flour
- 1 1/2 tsp baking powder
- 1/2 tsp baking soda
- 1/2 tsp salt
- 1 cup unsalted butter, softened
- 1 1/2 cups granulated sugar
- 3 large eggs
- 1/2 cup creamy peanut butter
- 1 tsp vanilla extract
- 1 cup milk
- 1 cup mini peanut butter cups, chopped

Ingredients for the frosting:

- 1 cup unsalted butter, softened
- 1 cup creamy peanut butter
- 4 cups powdered sugar
- 2 tbsp milk

Instructions:

1. Preheat oven to 350°F (175°C). Grease and flour two 9-inch round cake pans.
2. In a bowl, whisk together flour, baking powder, baking soda, and salt.
3. In a separate bowl, beat butter and sugar until light and fluffy. Add eggs one at a time, then stir in peanut butter and vanilla extract.
4. Gradually add dry ingredients, alternating with milk. Fold in chopped mini peanut butter cups.
5. Divide batter between pans and bake for 25-30 minutes.
6. For the frosting, beat peanut butter and butter until smooth. Gradually add powdered sugar and milk.
7. Frost the cooled cakes with peanut butter frosting.

Lemon Buttercream Cake

Ingredients for the cake:

- 2 cups all-purpose flour
- 1 1/2 tsp baking powder
- 1/4 tsp salt
- 1 cup unsalted butter, softened
- 1 1/2 cups granulated sugar
- 3 large eggs
- 1 tsp vanilla extract
- 1 tbsp lemon zest
- 1/2 cup fresh lemon juice
- 1/2 cup buttermilk

Ingredients for the frosting:

- 1 cup unsalted butter, softened
- 4 cups powdered sugar
- 2 tbsp fresh lemon juice
- 1 tsp vanilla extract

Instructions:

1. Preheat oven to 350°F (175°C). Grease and flour two 9-inch round cake pans.
2. In a bowl, whisk together flour, baking powder, and salt.
3. In a separate bowl, beat butter and sugar until fluffy. Add eggs one at a time, then stir in vanilla extract, lemon zest, and lemon juice.
4. Gradually add dry ingredients, alternating with buttermilk, until smooth.
5. Divide batter between pans and bake for 25-30 minutes.
6. For the frosting, beat butter and powdered sugar until smooth. Add lemon juice and vanilla extract.
7. Frost the cooled cakes with lemon buttercream.

Sweet Potato Cake

Ingredients for the cake:

- 2 cups all-purpose flour
- 1 1/2 tsp baking powder
- 1/2 tsp baking soda
- 1/2 tsp ground cinnamon
- 1/4 tsp ground nutmeg
- 1/2 tsp salt
- 1 cup cooked sweet potato, mashed
- 1 cup granulated sugar
- 1/2 cup unsalted butter, softened
- 3 large eggs
- 1 tsp vanilla extract
- 1/2 cup buttermilk

Ingredients for the frosting:

- 1 cup unsalted butter, softened
- 4 cups powdered sugar
- 1/2 tsp cinnamon
- 2 tbsp buttermilk
- 1 tsp vanilla extract

Instructions:

1. Preheat oven to 350°F (175°C). Grease and flour two 9-inch round cake pans.
2. In a bowl, whisk together flour, baking powder, baking soda, cinnamon, nutmeg, and salt.
3. In a separate bowl, beat butter and sugar until light and fluffy. Add eggs one at a time, then stir in mashed sweet potato and vanilla extract.
4. Gradually add dry ingredients, alternating with buttermilk, until smooth.
5. Divide batter between pans and bake for 25-30 minutes.
6. For the frosting, beat butter and powdered sugar until smooth. Add cinnamon, buttermilk, and vanilla extract.
7. Frost the cooled cakes with sweet potato frosting.

Pistachio Rose Cake

Ingredients for the cake:

- 2 cups all-purpose flour
- 1 1/2 tsp baking powder
- 1/4 tsp salt
- 1 cup unsalted butter, softened
- 1 1/2 cups granulated sugar
- 3 large eggs
- 1 tsp vanilla extract
- 1/4 cup ground pistachios
- 1/2 cup milk
- 1 tbsp rose water

Ingredients for the frosting:

- 1 cup unsalted butter, softened
- 3 cups powdered sugar
- 2 tbsp rose water
- 1/4 cup chopped pistachios for garnish

Instructions:

1. Preheat oven to 350°F (175°C). Grease and flour two 9-inch round cake pans.
2. In a bowl, whisk together flour, baking powder, and salt.
3. In a separate bowl, beat butter and sugar until fluffy. Add eggs one at a time, then stir in vanilla extract and rose water.
4. Gradually add dry ingredients, alternating with milk, and fold in ground pistachios.
5. Divide batter between pans and bake for 25-30 minutes.
6. For the frosting, beat butter and powdered sugar until smooth. Add rose water and mix.
7. Frost the cooled cakes with rose-flavored buttercream and garnish with pistachios.

Marble Cake

Ingredients for the cake:

- 2 cups all-purpose flour
- 1 1/2 tsp baking powder
- 1/2 tsp salt
- 1 cup unsalted butter, softened
- 1 1/2 cups granulated sugar
- 4 large eggs
- 1 tsp vanilla extract
- 1/2 cup milk
- 1/4 cup unsweetened cocoa powder
- 1/4 cup boiling water

Ingredients for the frosting:

- 1 cup unsalted butter, softened
- 3 cups powdered sugar
- 2 tbsp milk
- 1 tsp vanilla extract

Instructions:

1. Preheat oven to 350°F (175°C). Grease and flour two 9-inch round cake pans.
2. In a bowl, whisk together flour, baking powder, and salt.
3. In a separate bowl, beat butter and sugar until fluffy. Add eggs one at a time, then stir in vanilla extract.
4. Gradually add dry ingredients, alternating with milk, until smooth.
5. For the marble effect, mix cocoa powder and boiling water to create a paste, then swirl it into the batter.
6. Bake for 25-30 minutes.
7. For the frosting, beat butter and powdered sugar until smooth, then add milk and vanilla extract.
8. Frost the cooled cakes with vanilla buttercream.

www.ingramcontent.com/pod-product-compliance
Lightning Source LLC
LaVergne TN
LVHW081327060526
838201LV00055B/2496